Reforming Forwards?

The process of reception and the
consecration of women as bishops

Peter Toon

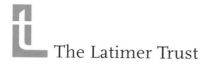

The Latimer Trust

Reforming Forwards?
The process of reception and the consecration of women as bishops

© 2004 by Peter Toon
ISBN 0 946307 50 4

Published by the Latimer Trust
PO Box 26685
London N14 4XQ

www.latimertrust.org

CONTENTS

Preface

Preface

It is a privilege and a joy to be associated once again with the name and work of the Latimer Trust. I was librarian at Latimer House in Oxford in the 1970s, working with Dr. Roger Beckwith, the warden at that time.

I spent a little over a decade in the United States of America where I was resident as a canon in the diocese of Quincy in the Episcopal Church, and involved in theological education and liturgical debate. Then, after 11 years, I returned to the Church of England in December 2001. My intention was to live quietly in a rural English parish, away from the many pressures of ministry in the American church. Though I lived quietly, before long I was called upon respond to various crises via e-mail. As a result of these crises, I urgently produced three publications in eighteen months to address contemporary questions in the Anglican family of churches.

First, *Neither Archaic nor Obsolete, The Language of Common Prayer and Public Worship* (Toon and Tarsitano: 2003) was written with Dr. Louis R. Tarsitano to be both a defence and a commendation of the traditional language of public prayer. At the time, the Episcopal Church planned to phase it out completely, and many parishes in the Church of England were being pressurised to use only 'contemporary language' on Sundays. Second, the longer study, *Common Worship Considered* (Toon: 2003), was written to provide a rational and critical comment on the content, problems, and weaknesses associated with the ever-growing directory of services in the Church of England that have been given the name *Common Worship*.

This essay on the process of reception was written out of a concern which developed as I helped several primates in 2001 to produce the book, *To Mend the Net: Anglican Faith and Order for Renewed Mission*, for the Primates' Meeting of that year. The same type of concern, albeit in a very different context, had been with me years earlier as I wrote *The Development of Doctrine in the Church*. The present concern may be put in this way: when it suits us, Anglicans pay lip service to the process of reception, which we understand imperfectly. Yet we do not seem to be ready to follow all its reasonably clear moral and practical implications. Thus, I attempt to show that the House of Bishops and the General Synod of the Church of England are fully committed by their public statements to this process, and further, I seek to point out the implications of that commitment for the future of the ordained ministry of women in the Church of England. I do this as The Working Party on Women in the Episcopate set up by the House of Bishops continues its work, which is, perhaps, directly contrary to the spirit of the process of reception.

So, this study is an attempt to explain the origins and the content of the process of reception as received by the Anglican Communion of Churches and by the Church of England, followed by an application of that process to the present state of the Church of England with regard to the ordained ministry of women. I am acutely aware that I run the risk, in expounding and applying the modern Anglican process of reception to the present state of the Church of England, of being misunderstood by both traditionalists and innovators alike. The innovators will not accept any hindering of what they consider progress, and the traditionalists will struggle with seeing beyond the use of the process of reception to my actual purpose, because they tend to see the process of reception as a political ploy dressed up as a theological position. However, those who read this booklet will see that I do give the process of reception the benefit of the doubt, and then attempt to take it seriously and to apply it forcefully. Whether we like it or not, the process of reception is part of the map of ecumenism and of Anglicanism in the twenty-first century.

Perhaps I need to explain that in Anglican theology there is in another meaning of reception and receptionism that relates to Holy Communion. The phrase, 'the doctrine of reception', has been used since at least the year 1867 to describe that view of the presence of Christ in the sacrament which locates the presence not in the elements of bread and wine, as in transubstantiation, but in the soul of the worthy receiver (see G.F. Cobb, *The kiss of peace: or, England and Rome at one on the doctrine of the Holy Eucharist*, 1867). I shall make no reference to this Eucharistic doctrine.

I want to express my thanks to the following persons for their help: my area bishop in the Diocese of Lichfield, Christopher Hill; Dr. Michael Nazir-Ali, Bishop of Rochester; Nigel Atkinson; Dr. Mark Burkill, Chairman of the Latimer Trust; Dr. Matthew Sleeman, theological secretary of the same trust; Dr. Louis Tarsitano; Ian Robinson; James Altena; Matthew Kennedy; Dr. Roger Beckwith; Dr. Timothy Bradshaw; and Vita Toon.

One book, *Seeking the Truth of Change in the Church* edited by Paul Avis, a collection of essays relating to the theme of reception, communion and the ordination of women, appeared after I wrote this booklet. Its most useful content does not cause me to change the basic argument of this essay concerning the Church of England and open reception therein.

I hope this study contributes to the genuine *koinonia* of the Spirit in the Church of England, and helps it discover and continue with what it has committed itself to in the process of reception with respect to the ordination of women.

The Rectory, Biddulph Moor, Stoke-on-Trent.

December 2003

Chapter One:

Reception, Testing, and Discernment

On 11 November 1992 the General Synod of the Church of England voted for the introduction of women as presbyters into the ordained ministry. The first women were ordained in 1994, after the *Priests (Ordination of Women) Measure* had been approved by Parliament and the Queen. During 1993, the House of Bishops and then the General Synod committed themselves to the new Anglican process of reception in their effort to prevent schism and to maintain communion within the divided national Church. Their commitment is visible in The Act of Synod of November 1993, and in the literature that shaped it. The ordination of women was publicised, while the adoption of the process of reception was merely an internal, ecclesiastical story, and even then a minor one. Yet adopting this process had profound implications, which only a few recognised at the time. Thus, our primary task in this study is to investigate the origins and content of the process of reception, together with the related doctrine of *koinonia* (communion), and to invite the House of Bishops to take seriously its own exposition of reception.

The ordination of women as deacons, as presbyters, and then as bishops within provinces of the Anglican Communion of Churches since the 1970s may be described either as an innovation in doctrine and order, or as a development through expansion of received doctrine and practice. Women had been deaconesses, heads of religious houses for women, heads of church schools, and had served as missionaries and evangelists, but never before (except in the isolated case of Florence Li Tim-Oi in Hong Kong from January 24, 1944, in World War II) had a woman been ordained into the threefold ministry in a jurisdiction of the one, holy, catholic, and

1

apostolic Church of God. When the decision to ordain women occurred, it did not represent the united mind of the provinces concerned, but only a majority in each of the provinces that took that step. The institution of the ordination of women created both elation and excitement on the one side, as well as deep feelings of division and alienation on the other throughout the Anglican family. These emotions became more obvious as the possibility of consecrating women as bishops became probable in the late 1990s.

The Process of Reception

In order to address this situation, at a late stage the Anglican Communion of Churches invented, or rather, adapted and utilised, the process of reception—a concept already known in western canon law, by historians of doctrine and adapted for use in ecumenical circles. Generally speaking, the process of reception refers to the way in which a doctrinal formulation or practice comes to be recognised within a church as being in harmony with the Gospel and the Christian tradition. By adopting and commending this new process of reception, along with an ecumenical doctrine of *koinonia* or communion, the leaders of the Anglican Churches hope to provide a solid basis for unifying both the proponents and the opponents of the ordination of women until general agreement of a positive or negative nature is reached by all, not only within the present 38 provinces, but by ecumenical partners as well. In passing, we need to note that the general tenor of the majority of the literature and of public statements by Anglicans seems to be that the result will probably be positive and thus eventually endorse the innovation.

The three key words inseparably connected to the process of reception with respect to the ordination of women are reception, testing, and discernment. **Reception** presumes that some women have been ordained in a diocese only after decisions to proceed have been made by a provincial synod. It becomes then the open and long-term process, involving attitude and action, within that province and related provinces of the church at all levels, of approving, accepting, and admitting (or in graciously not accepting and admitting) the presence of ordained women as presbyters and/or bishops (their presence as deacons seems not to be an issue). The acceptance is intended to be not minimal but to be concerned with real ministries of oversight, including the preaching of the word, the administration of the sacraments, and the exercise of discipline. And it is important to point out that it is the synodical decision and not the ministries of individual women that is the subject to the open process of reception.

Testing is an ongoing process within the provinces of the church at all levels and is composed of the informed responses by the faithful to the deployment of ordained women in pastoral leadership and as preachers of the word, celebrants of the sacraments, and administrators of discipline.

Discernment is the exercise of intellectual perception and insight within the process of testing. It should be guided by the Holy Spirit in order to judge whether this innovation of women in ordained ministry is of God, or is merely a sincere and rational response to human needs and aspirations. To exercise proper discernment and to ensure that there is some common ground, it is necessary to have agreement on a set of criteria as well as on the ways that the criteria are applied to the evidence found in the process of testing. As we shall see, while it was relatively easy to create the outlines of an Anglican process of reception with regard to the ordination of women, it is much more difficult to set criteria for (a) judging whether this phenomenon is of God, and (b) knowing when the actual process can be said to be complete and thus to have rendered its own clear and obvious results.

Perhaps an initial comment on the word 'reception' is appropriate here. Its adoption and use in the debate over the ordination of women does create a bias in some spheres, even if a small one, towards those in favour of the innovation. This is because the general use of the word in ordinary conversation is usually positive. Reception implies that something or someone is received, not rejected, and carries with it the same connotations associated with a reception room. Of course, it is now too late to change the word for another; however, we need to be aware of this bias, for it tends to give an advantage to the proponents of the innovation rather than its opponents.

The Anglican public use of the process of reception with regard to ordination can be traced to 1987. We shall explore the history of this term below, after we have noted the ecumenical context from which Anglicans gained the ingredients of their process of reception.

The Ecumenical Context

In the mid-1970s, few people in ecumenical circles were speaking of and writing about reception; yet, a decade later, it was becoming an important part of the vocabulary of the ecumenical movement. The important factors in this arousal of interest in reception included the dialogues and conversations between churches and denominations, the processes towards adopting common statements in their respective churches, and the Second Vatican Council and its aftermath. Further contributing factors included the entry of both the Orthodox Churches and the Roman Catholic Church into the ecumenical movement, the work of the Faith and Order Commission, and scholarly research concerning the ways in which doctrines and practices were received by the church in the patristic era and at the protestant reformation.

For the sake of clarity, it is useful to distinguish what may be called the classical concept of reception from the modern ecumenical concept of reception, bearing in mind that the latter is dependent upon the former. The Anglican process draws from both of these concepts, though it relies more heavily on the ecumenical concept. The classical idea of reception came to be part of traditional canon law. Here it refers to the acceptance by the local leadership and by the faithful, baptised membership of doctrines, dogmas, or hierarchical decisions that were handed down. Often, this handing down has been a simple process, especially where the local synods of bishops and the faithful see their duty as receiving that which comes to them from above (i.e., from an ecumenical council, a regional council or, in the West, from the Pope). The obvious examples are the Trinitarian dogma of the Ecumenical Councils of Nicea, Constantinople, and Chalcedon together with things such as the threefold ministry, the developed liturgy, and the canon of scripture. At best, reception is an active welcoming by the faithful rather than a passive acquiescence. Article VIII of *The Thirty-Nine Articles* declares, "the Three Creeds...ought thoroughly to be received and believed".

Of course, not everything passed by major regional councils or even from ecumenical councils was received wholly at the local levels. Sometimes reception meant 'No'! The best-known examples are the Christology of the Council of Chalcedon (451) in certain Eastern Churches and the *Filioque* in relation to the Nicene Creed in the East. Article XXI declares that "General Councils...may err, and sometimes have erred". Thus in the classical understanding, reception by the faithful is the final indication or sign that the doctrinal statements have fulfilled the necessary conditions for them to be a true expression of the faith. The people of God acknowledge the statements because in them they see the apostolic message and faith.

It is possible to speak of 'reception and re-reception' as 'the church's *Amen* to the word of God' as in *The Gift of Authority,* an Anglican - Roman Catholic International Commission [ARCIC] Statement of 1999:

> 24. Throughout the centuries, the Church receives and acknowledges as a gracious gift from God all that it recognises as a true expression of the Tradition which has been once for all delivered to the apostles. This reception is at one and the same time an act of faithfulness and of freedom...

> 25. There may be a rediscovery of elements that were neglected and a fresh remembrance of the promises of God, leading to renewal of the Church's "Amen".... This whole process may be termed *re-reception.*

Here there is no sense of innovation, but rather 'a rediscovery of elements that were neglected and a fresh remembrance of the promises of God.'

Ecumenical reception has for its context the divided church of the late-twentieth and early-twenty-first centuries, not the fundamentally united church of the first millennium. It is a process of separated churches and denominations within the World Council of Churches and the ecumenical movement receiving from each other: receiving, that is, not only agreed statements on doctrine and practice but also fellowship, mutual recognition of ministries, and a shared Eucharist. By such reception, churches and denominations, divided for centuries, are invited to reinterpret their heritage with new language as they recognise that they belong to the one ecumenical movement of the one body of Christ. Such reception is by its very nature filled with the possibility of great achievements as well as great pitfalls, and, while it has to be an open process, it is also a complicated and very long process, which is difficult at any point in space and time to assess. Its final goal is the uniting of divided churches.

William G. Rusch, a well-known Lutheran ecumenist and author of the small but most useful book, *Reception: An Ecumenical Opportunity* (1988), has attempted to offer a tentative definition of reception, which he believes includes:

> All phases or aspects of an ongoing process by which a church under the guidance of God's Spirit makes the results of a bilateral or multilateral conversation a part of its faith and life because the results are seen to be in conformity with the teaching of Christ and of the apostolic community, that is the gospel as witnessed to in Scripture. (p.31)

This definition recognises that ecumenical agreements come from outside the specific history and traditions of the participating churches and make claims upon them. It also acknowledges that the question raised by ecumenical reception for the churches is this: to what degree are they prepared to make authoritative within their own borders the results and conclusions of ecumenical dialogue? In other parts of his book, Rusch makes the additional point that 'response' to that which comes from outside is to be distinguished from reception, since the former is of a limited nature and duration whereas the latter is an open concept.

Responding to an ecumenical document by making resolutions in a synod to the intent that the document is commended for study is not reception as such, although it may be the beginning of the road to the same. Reception is the more demanding and comprehensive act and process wherein a doctrine or a rite, which is an innovation for the church concerned, is received and made a permanent part of the confession, belief and practice of that church. An example would be for a denomination to receive and use an ecumenical lectionary when it had not had one before. Another would be for a church to receive and use a set form of liturgy for use at the Lord's Supper when it had not had one before.

Apparently, the general structure and content of the doctrine of ecumenical reception originated from fertile dialogue at a time when there was enthusiastic cooperation amongst scholars from various backgrounds and churches in the ecumenical movement concerning the origins and development of doctrine in the church from the patristic period through to the seventeenth century. Some of the indications of the transfer and adaptation of the concept of reception from canon law and historical studies to the task and vocation of divided churches in the ecumenical movement can be seen, for those with time to peruse them, in the reports of the Commission on Faith and Order of the World Council of Churches between 1978 and 1984 (see Rusch, p.25ff). Thus, while the modern concept owes its name and origins to the classical concept, once it was articulated and accepted within the Faith and Order movement it began to have a life of its own, and that life is ongoing.

However, it is generally recognised that this ecumenical process was stalled for a decade or so. Reception by the churches of the results of consensus achieved in dialogue has proved more difficult than was expected in the 1980s. Part of the reason for this is that the institutions of conciliar ecumenism became largely captive to a new ecumenical paradigm that subordinated the concern of the Faith and Order movement for the visible unity of Christians to social and political agendas, which are divisive themselves. But more recently there have been successes in terms of mutual reception by churches in dialogue. In northern Europe the 1993 *Porvoo Common Statement,* involving Anglicans and Lutherans, is the best example. In this situation the expression 'differentiated consensus' is being increasingly used to describe the results of reception by and within the different but united churches.

In summary, and to use an illustration from Rusch, it may be said that the description of ecumenical dialogues and conversations may be likened to the discovery of new lands. Reception in this context is the opening up and the settlement of those lands, and such work takes time, patience, and effort, much more in fact than the original work of discovery.

The Lambeth Conference of 1988

The story of the specific Anglican (and the Church of England's) use of the concept of reception for its own internal reasons, in contrast to its use in ecumenical conversations with other churches, begins in the preparation for the Lambeth Conference of 1988 and is expressed in a variety of documents between 1988 and 2003. The primary cause for the origin of the Anglican process of reception was the very real possibility of the consecration of a woman as a bishop in the Episcopal Church in the United States of America [ECUSA].

Let us briefly note why the consecration of a woman raises greater problems for the church than does ordination to the presbyterate. It is commonly acknowledged that the bishop is the minister who maintains the unity of the church on three planes. He is the chief pastor, teacher, and minister of the sacraments in the diocese where he is a focus of unity; he is the one who, through his membership in the universal Episcopate, unites his diocese with other dioceses in the province, and the Catholic Church. He is the one who, through his consecration by three bishops, maintains the continuity of the episcopate in one place over time. A woman may be chosen, ordained, and consecrated for a diocese. Yet if there are priests and parishes therein who do not accept her, if there are bishops in other places who do not accept her, and if her ability to be in continuity with an all-male succession is seriously challenged, then on all three planes she is unable to function rightly as a bishop. Herein lies the reality of impaired communion in the province and in the Anglican Communion of Churches.

In 1994, *The Eames Commission: The Official Reports. The Archbishop of Canterbury's Commission on Communion and Women in the Episcopate* was published under the chairmanship of Robert Eames, Archbishop of Armagh and primate of all Ireland. Then, in 1998, a second edition entitled *Women in the Anglican Episcopate: Theology, Guidelines, and Practice* also contained the Monitoring Group Reports for 1995 to 1998. Both editions contain a message from Archbishop Carey, a statement on the origins of the Commission, and three reports of meetings, with four appendices. The origins of this Commission are to be directly traced to the Lambeth Conference of Anglican Bishops in 1988. In Resolution 1, that Conference resolved:

> (i) That each Province respect the decision and attitudes of other Provinces in the ordination or consecration of women to the episcopate, without such respect necessarily indicating acceptance of the principles involved, maintaining the highest degree of communion with the Provinces which differ.
>
> (ii) That bishops exercise courtesy and maintain communications with bishops who may differ, and with any woman bishop, ensuring an

open dialogue in the Church to whatever extent communion is impaired.

(iii) That the Archbishop of Canterbury, in consultation with the Primates, appoint a commission: a. to provide for an examination of the relationships between Provinces of the Anglican Communion and ensure that the process of reception includes continuing consultation with other Churches as well; b. to monitor and encourage the process of consultation within the Communion and to offer further pastoral guidelines.

The use of such words as 'respect,' 'courtesy,' and 'open dialogue' tends to make this resolution sound like an appeal based upon the best secular principles rather than on sure gospel virtues. The reference in paragraph 3 (above) to consultation with other churches is expanded a little in *The Report on Mission and Ministry* from the same Lambeth Conference. There we read that "the concept of reception has affected consideration of the ordination of women to the presbyterate and episcopate" and "in the process of reception the issue continues to be tested until it is clearly accepted or not accepted by the whole Church" (paragraph 133).

To see this reference to reception in context, we need to recall that there had been, in 1987, a working party of primates dealing with the question of the admission of women to the episcopate because it was expected that ECUSA would soon consecrate a woman. This working party provided an important and influential report to the 1988 Lambeth Conference. It is known as *Women and the Episcopate: The Grindrod Report* because it was chaired by John Grindrod, Archbishop of Brisbane. In this little-known report, the concept of reception, much in vogue in certain ecumenical conversations and debates, is apparently first officially applied to the subject of the ordination of women in the Anglican Communion.

The question arises as to whether it was the best concept to utilise for this purpose, since by its very nature and common-sense meaning, it appears to give advantage to the positive acceptance of the innovation. That is, reception seems to suggest that something or someone is actually received and admitted into the household. Yet if help for an Anglican problem was to be received from the ecumenical scene, then the concept of reception was present and waiting to be utilised. It had been used continuously for about a decade in ecumenical dialogues as well as within the Roman Catholic Church after the Second Vatican Council. A further possible attraction of this concept to Anglicans was that patristic studies have always been a major area of Anglican scholarship, and thus the classical idea of reception as the receiving by the local churches and faithful of the decisions of councils, however different from the ecumenical use of the term, was well known to scholars.

We must now return to the 1988 Lambeth Conference. In response to the conference's call, Archbishop Runcie appointed what was officially known as 'The Archbishop of Canterbury's Commission on Communion and Women in the Episcopate' but became known as 'The Eames Commission'. The Commission met four times between November 1988 and March 1990, and then once more (at the request of the new Archbishop of Canterbury, George Carey) in 1993. It produced three reports, one on the first two meetings, another on the next two meetings, and then one on the last meeting. In the next chapter we shall examine the exposition of the process of reception contained in these reports, as well as that of the Eames Monitoring Group Report of August 1997.

Chapter Two:

The Eames Commission

The mandate of the Eames Commission from the start of its work in November 1988 was 'to discover how Anglicans may live in the highest possible degree of communion with the existence of differences of principle and practice on the ordination of women to the episcopate'. Its task was 'to try to discover the language and context in which Anglicans can continue to live together'. Therefore, it came to see the study of communion (*koinonia*) as central to its work, and made use of the Anglican concept of reception already articulated in *The Grindrod Report*.

Since taking up the process of reception in *The Grindrod Report* may be seen as the articulation of a specifically Anglican use of this ecumenical doctrine, it will be appropriate to quote from it before moving on to the reports from the Eames Commission. Making reference to a possible, impending decision to consecrate a woman to the episcopate in a context where women were already being ordained as presbyters in some provinces, Grindrod stated:

> 85. However, at the present time, if a decision is to be made, the only effective level at which it can be made is at the Provincial level with due regard to consultation with all the Provinces through the A[nglican] C[onsultative] C[ouncil] and the Lambeth Conference and with due listening to sister churches. Should a Province, after due consultation, proceed to consecrate a woman as a bishop then that decision would still have to be tested in the universal Church. As with other developments of faith and order such a development would have to be affirmed by the people of God under the guidance of the Holy Spirit. A long-range and far-reaching process of reception by the whole Church would lie ahead. Until a process of reception is reasonably settled the issue of the ordination of women to the episcopate, as indeed the ordination of women to the presbyterate, would remain open to discussion. A continuing discussion between Provinces and

between churches in the ecumenical movement would be appropriate. We are already in bilateral and multilateral conversations with our sister churches and look forward to exchanges on the subject. It might be possible for some who remain agnostic, or who are even opposed to the consecration of women, to remain in communion with Provinces that consecrated women, and even to share collegially with women, providing all understand the practice within the perspective of such a continuing and open process of reception. However, it needs to be recognised that there is a very particular problem when what is being put to the test in the reception process is not just a doctrine to be discussed, but a doctrine that is already embodied in persons which touch and affect the very bond of communion. (p.9)

Here we see a process of reception with regard to the ordination of women to the episcopate shaped within an ecumenical context of 'bilateral and multilateral conversations,' an Anglican context that is both international and provincial (e.g., the Anglican Consultative Council), and the human context of 'embodied in persons'. We see also the expression of the hope that Anglicans will find a way to stick together when the innovation occurs and the boat is severely rocked. Further, we notice that the process of reception is envisaged as a long, open, and difficult process. All these themes will remain in focus and be articulated by those who prepare reports and papers on this topic during the next fifteen years or so.

A possible interpretation of this early stage in the Anglican use of the concept of reception is that there was a crisis looming in the Anglican family of churches, and as its leaders sought to find a way through and to keep everybody on board they looked around and seized upon the fertile notion of reception. This concept was being used widely and creatively in the ecumenical movement, and it had not yet reached any state of agreed content or application. Thus, it was sufficiently in a state of development, even of flux, and was adaptable to the peculiar Anglican need. *The Grindrod Report* emphasised the importance of 'the theological concept of reception':

> 90. It is not in the remit of the Working Party to make recommendations either for or against the ordination of women to the episcopate. However, we have constantly been struck by the importance of the theological concept of reception. We note that in the case of the admission of Gentiles to the Church and the matter of circumcision Paul's actions in one part of the expanding Church were in advance of the decision of the whole Church. However, before this was determined to be right it had to be agreed by the 'Apostles, Elders and the whole Church' (Acts 15). Similarly, in the definition of orthodox teaching it took centuries before the mind of the whole Church was expressed by Councils in the formation of the Creeds. Nearer our own day the fruits of ecumenical dialogues, in particular the substantial agreements of the *Final Report* of the A[nglican] R[oman] C[atholic] I[nternational] C[omission] and *Baptism, Eucharist and Ministry* (the Lima Text) are involving Anglicans, and all the participating churches, in a process of reception. Beyond the official response process involving the Provinces and the articulation of the mind of the Communion through the Lambeth Conference lies a continuing process of reception by the Church. Moreover, in this process what is affirmed in words has to be embodied in the life of the Church if the reception is to be credible. (p.14)

The classic concept of reception, which relates primarily to the receiving of the doctrines of councils or synods, was difficult to apply to the Anglican situation, since individual provinces prized their autonomy and were prepared to go ahead with innovations. They believed that other provinces would eventually follow their example or leave them in peace. There was no possibility for having an international, *authoritative* council with appropriate powers to formulate an agreed doctrine on women's ministry that would be offered to the provinces. So, if reception was to be used it had to be in the form of the modern concept, which was sufficiently pliable to be made serviceable to pressing Anglican needs. There is reference in paragraph 90, cited above, to the process of reception with respect to modern ecumenical agreements.

Just how deeply and profoundly the members of the Eames Commission thought about, discussed, and considered this novel ecumenical doctrine for a novel Anglican situation, we do not know. The evidence is that they made wide use of it as they received it from the Grindrod Report. However, whether or not they significantly developed the concept past the point at which the Grindrod Report left it is not certain. One thing can be said, that the Eames Commission sought to tie together the process of reception and the ecumenical doctrine of *koinonia*.

The First Report

The first report from the Eames Commission covers the first two meetings, held in November 1988 and March 1989, and it has five brief chapters. In chapter III, 'Koinonia and the Anglican Communion,' the subject of reception is first raised in the context of the existence of a divided mind within a provincial synod as the synod prepared for the vote concerning the ordination of women at the synod. The Commission stated, in reference to what happens after a majority decision has been taken, "We believe a proper understanding of the process of discernment and reception is of particular significance" (III. 41). This process involves all sides respecting the decision of the synod while recognising that 'councils not only may, but have erred.' Conciliar and synodical decisions would still have to be received and owned by the whole people of God as consonant with "the faith of the church throughout the ages professed and lived today" (III. 42). Further, "in the continuing and dynamic process of reception, freedom and space must be available until a consensus of opinion one way or another has been achieved"

(III. 43). There is great emphasis upon courtesy and respect as the best of human virtues in the way that arguments are presented and people treat each other. Further, the Commission was firm in its statement that the process is an open one:

> The fact that a synod has reached a decision does not foreclose the matter. Both sides need to work hard to ensure that the process of reception continues to be as open as possible, recognising that synodical decisions may indeed come to be overwhelmingly affirmed or on the other hand, equally as overwhelmingly rejected. A real commitment to the maintenance of the highest degree of communion implies that there must be some limit to the expression of dissent in the life of the Church. In this process of reception, bishops in particular have a special responsibility to be sensitive both to the mind of the synod and to the collegiality of the house of bishops. (III. 44)

The Commission was well aware of the ecumenical dimensions. "It is particularly important that the process of reception should not be foreclosed. The lack of an agreement on this matter with our ecumenical partners should alert us to the provisionality of the decision making process in Anglican Provinces and even in inter-Anglican organs of consultation" (III. 46). In the final paragraph of chapter III, the Commission presented a series of questions as criteria for discerning whether or not a development such as the ordination of women is authentic:

> Does it enhance the fidelity of that particular church to the Gospel?

> Does it enable that church to fulfil its mission more faithfully in its own cultural context?

> Does the development affect holiness of life, both for individuals and for communities?

> Does the church continue to be seen as the body of Christ, where the Gospel is proclaimed and believers are nurtured in fellowship and in truth?

Are there necessary elements of continuity with the Church in other ages and different cultures? (III. 47)

No attempt was made to define the meaning of these questions or to begin to answer them. Further, the fact that the Commission consistently referred to 'the development' rather than to 'the innovation' of the ordained ministry of women weights the scales in favour of the new phenomenon in any application of the criteria. In the final two chapters of the first report, there are suggestions and guidelines offered on the practical reality of maintaining communion within dioceses and between provinces, once there are women presbyters and bishops ministering in them.

One gets the impression from reading the first report that the Commission was seeking to be fair to both sides in the controversy, was desirous of finding means that would enable all to remain in respectful fellowship and co-operation, and did not want to suggest that the 'innovation' or 'development' is necessarily here to stay forever. Yet the attempt to offer criteria by which to judge whether the process be of God or of man seems rather weak, and appears as a kind of afterthought or an act of desperation. It is one thing to call for respect, to state that synods may err, and to insist that reception is an open process; it is yet another to set out carefully defined criteria and to offer sound methods by which to apply the criteria to the complex ecclesial reality. Thus, after studying this report, it is disappointing that the process seems hardly to have moved on from the Grindrod positions.

The Second Report

The second report covers the third meeting, held in October 1989, and it has eight short chapters. Many of the contents of the report are responses to the earlier report from the primates' meeting held in Cyprus in May 1989 and from the provinces. There is also a brief report on 'ecumenical evidence' especially concerning *koinonia*.

In terms of the process of reception, we learn that the Commission's comments about 'provisionality', paragraph 21 in its first report, had raised the most questions amongst the primates and provinces. In seeking to clarify this matter the Commission wrote:

> Our admission of a degree of provisionality to the development of the ordination of women has sometimes been misunderstood as saying that the ministry of women is unfruitful or that they have only provisionally been ordained. This is not the case. No judgement is being passed upon the ministry of ordained women as such. What is being maintained is that within an open process of reception there is inevitably a provisionality about the *development* itself. (VI. 34)

Of course, had the Commission used the word 'innovation' of women's ordination then their meaning would have been clearer from the beginning. What is clear from the first report is the real possibility that the innovation may be judged eventually to be of man, not of God, and thus be disbanded. In this context, the present ministry of women as ordained persons must be reckoned as an experiment rather than as a permanent feature of the threefold ministry. But to use the word 'experiment', as to use the word 'provisionality', is to raise emotions and risk the loss of reasoned discourse.

In the seventh chapter there are recommendations for further study by an inter-Anglican theological/doctrinal commission. These include such subjects as the autonomy and interdependence of provinces, the relationship between revelation and the task of mission, and the relationship between communion and truth (a topic taken up by the Inter-Anglican Theological and Doctrinal Commission and set forth in the 1998 *Virginia Report*). In regard to reception the following is stated:

> Given the New Testament understanding of revelation as an eschatological reality and that now we "see, as through a glass, dimly not face to face", it is important to be aware of the incomplete nature of our perceptions of God and his will for his Church. The process of reception of a doctrine or practice within the life of the Church needs further study from this eschatological perspective. This would include an examination of the authoritative role of synods in decision-making, the doctrine of development, and the place of praxis in the process of discernment and reception. (VII. 39)

Here what is called for are major studies whose findings, however relevant, would be controversial and which would hardly help with the actual testing and discerning of the process of the ordination and deployment of women as clergy in the short term. We shall note in the next chapter how the bishops of the Church of England in 2000 take up the theme of incomplete perception of God and his will in relation to the Act of Synod.

The second report also covered the fourth meeting of the Eames Commission held in London in March 1990, and this has seven short chapters. While there are occasional references to reception, the main thrust relates to the practical guidelines for and details of maintaining communion where there is division over the consecration and ministry of a woman bishop.

The Third Report

The Commission was reconvened for a meeting in London in December 1993. By this time there were four women bishops (three in ECUSA and one in New Zealand) and many women presbyters across the Anglican Commission, although women in the Church of England had to wait until 1994 for the first ordinations in England. This report has four chapters; the third is entitled 'Reception'. This chapter summarised the latest thinking of members of the commission on this topic, the members recognising that it was being discussed and utilised in ecumenical conversations. However, they conflated what has been called the ecumenical (modern) concept of reception, which deals with the acceptance of doctrines and practices between denominations in modern times and which 'is a continuous process' with the classical idea of reception, as used by historians of doctrine to deal with the acceptance of the decisions of councils and synods in the whole life of the church. Nevertheless, they did readily concede that "the process of receiving the Gospel is neither effortless nor painless" (III. 37).

Referring to the period of the early church in the apostolic era and afterwards, the Commission wrote:

> As the Church's life continued, so did the process of reception. For example, the development of the Logos theology to make sense of the presence and work of Christ in the world had to be received by the Christian community and commended to others. Over time and through a process of discernment, the Church came to affirm the decisions of the councils of Nicea and Constantinople. Yet the most obvious example of reception was the inclusion of gentiles in the early Church. (III. 38)

To these examples others could be added: the reception of the canon of scripture, both the Old and of the New Testaments; of the Eucharist as the Sunday service of the ministry of word and sacrament; of the threefold ministry; and of the patriarchates in Alexandria, Antioch, Jerusalem, Constantinople, and Rome. Of all the processes given as examples, one thing may be said: they did not happen overnight. The process of reception took a long time, often a very long time. Speaking generally, the Commission stated:

The process of reception in the Church can be difficult and time-consuming. There is no pre-determined result. A matter for reception arises when a local situation demands response. When it touches the life of the wider Church, it needs to be considered at the appropriate level of the Church. However, even when a synodical or conciliar body makes a decision, there is still need of further discernment by the faithful that the matter is consonant with the Apostolic Faith. (III. 40)

It added:

Nevertheless, because we are part of the One, Holy, Catholic and Apostolic Church, reception is never a matter for each tradition in isolation. It is incumbent upon us to offer our developing insights in dialogue with Christians of other traditions. (III. 41)

However, it also emphasised (probably recalling the Lambeth Quadrilateral of 1888):

To talk of a continuous process of reception in the life of the Church is not to deny that there are some things which remain constant in its life. The truth of the Gospel is grounded in the canon of Scripture, the teaching set forth in the Catholic Creeds, the Apostolic Ministry and the sacramental life of the Church. These fundamentals are matters received by the Church for all time. (III. 42)

This part ends with yet another call for maintaining communion. "During the process of reception, we need to make space for each other and to listen to each other in charity and patience while remaining in the highest possible degree of communion in spite of difference, as we strive to be open to the insights of the wider Christian community" (III. 43).

In the next chapter, the Commission recognised that the process will be a long one:

Without predicting the outcome, the process of reception throughout the Anglican Communion is likely to last a very long time. Thus as a Communion we will need to become accustomed to living with ambiguities within our ministry. Such ambiguities bring pain and confusion, but are the mark of a living, if suffering, church that remains bound by the dispersal of legislative authority through the provincial churches. (IV. 47)

Whether the concept of reception as found in the reports of the Eames Commission can be called coherent is debatable. While there is much emphasis upon testing and discernment in an open situation and communicants are urged to live in the highest possible degree of communion with one another, the real problem is that clarity about the precise criteria for testing and discerning in this fluid and complex situation is not provided anywhere. Further, though it is constantly stated that it is an open process and that the end result is not known, the whole situation of reception seems in reality to be partially closed and going in one direction only, particularly in those provinces where women are being ordained in ever larger numbers.

The Fourth Report

The Eames Monitoring Group report was concluded in 1997 in time for the Lambeth Conference of 1998. It has eight short chapters and one of these, Chapter VI, is entitled 'Reception.' This chapter begins with the observation that "the part that reception plays in the life of the Church has been fundamental to the way in which the Anglican Communion has understood itself wrestling with the question of the ordination of women to the presbyterate and episcopate." Then, for the first time in any of the Eames Commission's reports there is mention of *The Grindrod Report* followed by long quotations from it. We have cited this report already, but it is worth adding this paragraph on the consecration of women to the episcopate:

93. The episcopate is not the possession of an individual Province but belongs to the Church. Therefore any decision regarding the fundamental expression of the episcopate would need ultimately to be

affirmed by the Church. Those Provinces which are convinced that it is right to consecrate a woman as bishop may wish to exercise restraint because of the possible disruptive effects upon the Communion. Alternatively, they may be persuaded by compelling doctrinal reasons, by their experience of women in ordained ministry and by the demands of the mission of the Church in their region to proceed to the ordination of a woman to the episcopate. This would be done only with overwhelming support in the diocese concerned. Such a step could only be taken within an over-riding acknowledgement of the need to offer such a development for reception, or indeed rejection, by the whole Communion and by the universal Church and with care and support for the women concerned. (p.116)

Chapter VI ends on a positive note by expressing the view that the process of reception seems to be working, and that it is developing in an open and tolerant way.

Evaluation

In hindsight, it may reasonably be claimed that the Anglican Communion has not given enough consideration to the fact that the evolving concept of ecumenical reception referred to and covered very different ground than that addressed by the evolving Anglican process of reception. In the ecumenical sphere, there is agreement by a joint commission on some doctrine that is believed to be rooted in scripture, and then that doctrine is introduced into one or all of the participating churches from outside. On the inside, it meets varied responses at different levels, and if successful, is eventually received by the synod or governing body and made part of the actual heritage of faith and order that belongs to and defines that church. Here the acceptance by a synod is the mature result of the process of reception. In contrast, reception in the Anglican sphere of women's ordination relates very much to what follows the majority decision of the synod of a church (that is, by a particular province) to innovate. There is no sense of recovering a lost doctrine or practice, but rather the sense of starting something new which is perceived of as good for all and as not contrary to the teaching of the Bible. Then the faithful in a province, as well as the faithful elsewhere, are asked to receive that which is passed by majority vote within the synod of the one province. So, one way of describing this Anglican method is 'reforming forwards.'

The term 'reforming forwards' captures what may be an inherent flaw in the Anglican 'doctrine of reception'. The oldest test of validity in Christianity is antiquity. The New Testament constantly invokes the Old Testament to validate its account of Christ or the applications of its doctrine. Similarly, the test for inclusion in the New Testament canon was apostolic authority, the past guaranteeing the present. Vincent of Lerins really only clarified this 'test by antiquity' with his 'everywhere, always, and by all' (*Commonitorium*, 3.4, AD434). Just as Irenaeus of Lyons in the second century AD looked back to apostolic authority and the ancient sees, Vincent also would have seen any departure from established truth and precedent as heresy, that is, as a personal choice imposed upon the faith and the household of God.

Sometimes the identification of a council as 'general' has been described as reception, but in this case the word is not being used in the same way as the current process of reception. When a council issued its decrees, church people in their various local jurisdictions were expected to confirm or deny that the members of the council had remained consistent with the received doctrine and practice of the church. If they confirmed a council, they 'received' it in the sense that they recognised the council as not departing from the faith once delivered. This perspective, of course, was based once again on the use of the past in evaluating and confirming the present.

The official documents of the English Reformation were very careful to invoke the authority of the past as justification for the reforming actions. It was stipulated repeatedly that no departure from the Catholic faith was intended, and that the changes being made were either clarifications of past doctrine or an actual return to ancient faith and practice. The justification of the English Prayer Book was that it was the Book of the Common Prayer of the whole church, in the form intended for use in the realm of England. Furthermore, King Henry's original authority to pursue reformation was justified by the example of Constantine's imperial authority to convene a council of the lands under his rule.

In its present form, Anglican reception is not an appeal to the sureties of the past, or even to what has been. Instead, it is an appeal to what might be someday, with the associated permission to test or experiment with the proposed possibilities of the future. This kind of reception is thus a novelty in itself. It is no longer a 'reformation' (an effort to achieve the original, pristine form). Rather it is a 'reformation forwards,' implying that the true form of the church may not have been seen or achieved yet. This is not, however, an eschatological consideration declaring that we are not altogether sure what Christ will make of us. Rather, it is an inversion, an experiment to determine what we will discover of Christ and his body, the church.

In the end, one is faced with this question: is there justification provided in the scriptures for a principle of experimentation? No previous effort at reformation or renewal has looked to the future, rather than to the settled past. It may even be said that the reformation forward is contrary to every basic principle of church polity. For the experiment to proceed, it must be permitted by human authority; however, until the experiment succeeds, it cannot be known if the human authorities granting permission have the divinely given authority to allow the experiment. In this way, it seems that those who engage in the modern form of Anglican receptionism are permitting what they are not sure they can permit, until God either rewards them or punishes them for it. The normal order of revelation is reversed, in that man is acting ahead of God's 'thus saith the Lord,' rather than in response to it. To put it another way, the church is acting first and deciding later, contrary to the natural order of events that has been followed hitherto. Waiting for a favourable decision before acting certainly is frustrating, but failing to wait stores up trouble for the future.

Even if these considerations are stated too strongly, I, for one, cannot avoid having serious misgivings about modern Anglican receptionism. The classical concept of reception holds that whatsoever is proposed to be received must be entirely consonant with all that has been received previously (i.e., it is elaborative and/or supplemental). The modern concept explicitly allows that whatever is proposed to be received may contradict, overrule, and supplant that which previously has been received. This said, it is a fact of our common life, and an amazing one at that, that this particular understanding of reception has been adopted by the primates of the Anglican Communion and by the provinces. As dutiful members, we are all expected to do our best to make sense of it. Further, we should see to it that those who invoked it honour it in its application, and so ease or even justify the entrance of these sorts of innovations into the life of the Anglican family of churches. In this spirit, we turn next to the adoption and statement of the concept of reception by the House of Bishops of the Church of England.

Chapter Three:

Reception, a Process of the Church of England

In this chapter, we turn to the use of the concept of reception by the Church of England since the early 1990s. Much of this use is in connection with the provisions made by the General Synod for those who had objections to the ordination of women as presbyters. *The Episcopal Ministry Act* was passed by the General Synod at its November sessions in 1993 to make provision for the continuing diversity of opinion in the Church of England concerning the ordination and ministry of women. The canon to allow the ordination of women as presbyters had been passed on 11 November 1992.

Before looking at the contents of this Act, it is necessary to do two things: to notice what is the legal status of an Act of Synod, and to note two documents produced by the House of Bishops in preparation for it. These documents, *The Manchester Statement* and *Bonds of Peace*, were both written in 1993. The latter document contains the draft of the subsequent Act. We all need to be clear that an Act of Synod is simply and only that. It is something passed by a majority vote in the General Synod, and as such it can be overturned at any later time by a majority vote. It is not surprising that active feminists inside and outside of the Synod are calling, in 2003, for its withdrawal. In contrast, what is known as *The Priests (Ordination of Women) Measure 1993* has the force of law and cannot be overturned by the General Synod, except with the approval of Parliament and the Monarch.

The Two Documents

The Manchester Statement followed a House of Bishops meeting in the city of Manchester in January 1993. In it, there is an attempt to state what kind of arrangements would be necessary after the institution of the ordination of women as priests to ensure continued Episcopal oversight and pastoral care for all the members of the Church of England. In their exposition, the bishops reveal their commitment to the process of reception and their use of the reports of the Eames Commission. "We all recognise that the vote of the General Synod must be seen as part of a wider process within the Church of England, within the Anglican Communion and within the universal Church in which the question of women's ordination to the priesthood is being tested."

They recognise the rightful place in the church of those who oppose the ordination of women and they encourage a willingness on the part of all to listen respectfully to the views of those with whom they differ. The bishops continue:

> We believe that the Anglican ethos and tradition which has been developed under God through our experience and history gives us particular resources for living through our present disagreements and uncertainties and of doing so together. This ethos, tradition and communion include commitment to Biblical authority, Trinitarian worship, respect for traditional doctrinal formulations, agreement about the need for an ordered and ordering ministry, and the practice of mutual responsibility and fellowship of a particularly open kind. Although we have differing interpretations, views and practices we maintain a shared commitment to belong together and to serve God together. (p.2)

After outlining their proposals for continued episcopal oversight and care, the bishops state that the arrangements "involve a willingness on the part of all to act sensitively and flexibly, with full recognition of the integrity of those who hold differing views on the ordination of women to the priesthood. We believe that they [the arrangements] will ensure the maximum degree of communion between those of differing views while allowing the space which is necessary if this diversity is to be maintained within a framework of legitimate order."

Finally, on the matter of communion they write:

> There are many aspects of communion; it is not an all-for-nothing state of relationship. Even when full sacramental communion may be restricted, members of the Church of England will continue to participate in the common goods of a shared baptism, shared faith, shared history, shared mission, and shared material resources and responsibilities. If different traditions are to continue alongside one another in fruitful interchange, it is essential that those who belong to them should play their full part at parish, deanery, diocesan and national level as far as conscience allows. (p.4)

In *Bonds of Peace*, a somewhat longer statement that followed a June 1993 meeting that was also held in Manchester, the House of Bishops dealt with arrangements for pastoral care following the ordination of women to the priesthood. It freely admitted that "discernment of the matter is now to be seen within a much broader and longer process of discernment within the whole Church under the Spirit's guidance." The bishops also explained:

> We now enter a process in which it is desirable that both those in favour and those opposed should be recognised as holding legitimate positions while the whole Church seeks to come to a common mind. The Church of England needs to understand itself as a communion in dialogue, committed to remaining together in the ongoing process of the discernment of truth within the wider fellowship of the Christian Church. Giving space to each other, and remaining in the highest degree of communion in spite of differences are crucial, as we strive to be open to the insights of the wider Christian community. Though some of the means by which communion is expressed may be strained or broken, the need for courtesy, tolerance, mutual respect, prayer for one another, and a continuing desire to know one another and to be with one another, remain binding on us as Christians, no less within our own Church than is already the case in our ecumenical relations. The danger to be avoided is that, where ecclesial communion is impaired, communities may begin to define

themselves over against one another and develop in isolation from one another. (p.3)

The bishops went on to state that "those who for a variety of reasons cannot conscientiously accept that women may be ordained as priests will continue to hold a legitimate and recognised position within the Church of England" and "the bishops, corporately and individually, are pledged to maintain the integrity of both positions."

The Act

In the light of these two documents, it is not surprising that in the preliminaries to this Act the General Synod states that all concerned should endeavour to ensure that:

(i) discernment in the wider Church of the rightness or otherwise of the Church of England's decision to ordain women to the priesthood should be as open a process as possible;

(ii) the highest possible degree of communion should be maintained within each diocese;

(iii) the integrity of differing beliefs and positions concerning the ordination of women to the priesthood should be mutually recognised and respected.

Here, very clearly, is an appeal for unity based upon the concept of reception from the Eames Commission as received by the House of Bishops and then by the Synod. Thus it may be claimed that the Anglican process of reception has become a foundational doctrine for the way in which women are to be ordained and deployed in the Church of England. This doctrine has implications for the Church that stretch far into the future, only one of which is the question of whether or not the Church decides to move ahead with a measure to consecrate women as bishops.

At this stage in 1993, the General Synod was prepared to state that the decision to ordain women may be a wrong one. There was a call for discernment to judge whether the decision is right or wrong and for that discernment to be as open a process as possible. However, there was no indication at all as to how many years this open process is expected to take or should be allowed to take. The Synod followed the House of Bishops in calling for the highest possible degree of communion to be maintained during the process. Further, the Synod called for those on both sides to recognise the integrity not only of their own position, but that of their opponents.

Report of a Working Party

In the *Report of a Working Party of the House of Bishops* of 2000 on the 1993 Act of Synod, there are, in Chapter 2, various observations on the concept of reception, with reference to both the Eames Reports and to *Being in Communion*, the Statement of the House of Bishops of June 1993. The report declares, "the Church is engaged in a fluid and dynamic process, with and towards God, in which it perceives but dimly God's will and created order. This is not a weakness to be corrected but rather the natural corollary of being a new creation in Christ (2 Cor 5:17), and yet still part of the old creation" (2:4). Then, under the heading of 'Discernment/Reception' it explains:

> The ordination of women as priests must be understood in the context of this fluid and dynamic process. It is a process of discernment to which all are called, and in which all are expected to act with Christian charity as they endeavour to receive God's grace. Such an emphasis upon *reception* is important because, as already stated, the Church receives the sacrament of ordination as a gift, and therefore understands ministry in the light of its relationship with God. Correctly understood, that relationship is always conditioned by God:

all we can do is to work towards its truthful interpretation in the light of the Church's tradition and present situation in the world. (2:5)

Here we are told that we have very limited insight into the mind and will of God and thus all are engaged in a process of seeking to clarify what is that mind and will with respect to the specific topic of ordination. Until the middle of the twentieth century, the church believed, confessed and taught with clarity on this topic; but since then, its vision has become clouded as it perceives that it might have been living in ignorance during the centuries when it lived with clarity on this topic. The changed position of women in society has certainly caused the church to reflect upon its received doctrine and to be prepared to develop and change it.

It is not wholly clear whether the report's references to 'process' are in any way related to process theology, wherein it is taught that God as God is involved in an evolutionary process together with the world, and that even as the world is developing, so also is God.

Then in 2:6, the first report of the Eames Commission is visited for three quotations in order to make three points. First, a proper understanding of the process of discernment and reception is significant and is required. Second, synodical decisions on this matter should be respected by all but, at the same time, it is recognised that councils may err. Third, in the process of reception, freedom and space must be available to all until a consensus of opinion is reached.

In 2:7, the point is made that the Church of England as an individual church could have got the matter wrong in its vote for women's ordination. For the decision to be known to be right it has to be received by the universal church. Thus in 2:8, it is admitted that no-one can say how long the process of reception is likely to take. If, after a long period, there is no consensus for the ordination of women, then the wisdom of the decision made in 1992 must be called into question. So, this part of Chapter 2 ends by counselling the people in the Church to content themselves humbly and patiently to be ignorant before God.

It is of great importance to the present situation of the Church of England that this working party acknowledged that the period of reception is still ongoing. Further, if we think of the process as including not only the Anglican Communion of Churches but also the Orthodox and Roman Catholic churches, there is the possibility that this doctrine and its subsequent ministerial innovation will never be received by a majority of the Church of God on earth. The working party does not, however, look at the question as to whether the Church of England should continue to ordain women as presbyters and plan to ordain them as bishops when it fully confesses that the process is still ongoing and reception is very far from complete. It is perhaps reasonable to suggest that the more women who are ordained the more will it look to many people as though the question is being settled by the weight of numbers. On the other hand, if the consensus of the universal church is eventually clear and is negative, then where great numbers of women have been ordained and deployed there will have to be a massive operation to undo what has been done and to find ways of deploying the women in alternative forms of ministry. Surprisingly, the question that is *not* raised is this: why not have a limited number of women admitted into Holy Orders in the period of reception so that the experiment does not get out of hand? In fact, the fewer ordained women there are, the smaller the problem of impaired communion in the Church of England will be.

The penultimate part of Chapter 2, sections 2:14-16, takes up the theme of 'impaired communion,' which refers not to the relationship of a repentant sinner to God himself, but to members of the one body of Christ who are divided over the issue of women in orders. It is rightly stressed that all baptised Christians have a basic and fundamental unity in Christ because of their baptism, and so they are in communion one with another. However, the full experience of this communion is argued as known in the Holy Communion or Eucharist. Yet where a woman priest is the celebrant, some persons, male and female, will be unable to communicate, for they do not believe that she is a true presbyter/priest and thus cannot be a genuine celebrant of the holy mysteries. In the process of reception, this state of affairs will often be present and it is the duty of all involved to maintain the highest level of respect and good manners in Christian love (as the House of Bishops had encouraged).

The final sections, 2:17-19, deal with the theme of integrity in order to explain it, and in so doing, to reject the idea of integrities. "The theology of the 1993 Act supports the conviction that more than one position on the ordination of women as priests may be held *with integrity*. What this means is that, during a period of discernment, people of differing beliefs and positions may honourably hold those views, whilst sharing one communion" (2:17). In 2:18 it is claimed: "To attempt to distinguish between that one integrity, or worse, to speak of 'two integrities,' is to depart from a correct understanding of God's gift to the world."

The report is correct to insist that there is one integrity only. However, in the rough and tumble of parish, deanery, and diocesan activities there seems to be a great gulf fixed between the dedicated feminist understanding of women in the ministry representing the 'feminine within God and Christ,' and the traditional Catholic understanding of the male priest as standing in the place of Christ, the incarnate

God as male. Each certainly holds its opinion with conviction and believes that it has integrity as a consistent and necessary doctrine.

In fact, if one reviews the use of the word 'integrity' in the two 1993 statements of the House of Bishops, one can see that what is being claimed in 2000 is the result of continued reflection upon that use and is not precisely what was stated in 1993. Further, one cannot help but observe that much of the talk about integrity simply equates integrity with a certain consistency of basic assumptions and practice. By that standard, any consistent system, even Nazism, can be said to have integrity. We may recall that the only genuine integrity for Christians is that which conforms to divine order and relation, and is thus integrated by divine intention and design.

In reviewing the second chapter of the *Report of the a Working Party of the House of Bishops* we have passed over the three paragraphs, 2:11-13, which deal with the diocesan bishop as the ordinary (the one who has oversight in his own right and not by deputation, that is, he has immediate jurisdiction). It is stated emphatically that the bishop to whom the care of a diocese is given must exercise that care, for it is given to him not by man, but by God. Thus, if he chooses to ask another bishop (assistant, neighbouring, or a Provincial Episcopal Visitor) to help him in this pastoral care for parishes that hold a different position to him on the ordination of women, it is to be seen as *extended* episcopal oversight, not alternative oversight. The House of Bishops has stated this point with vigour in *Being in Communion*:

> 23. Oversight remains ultimately with the Diocesan Bishop, who remains the focus of unity in his diocese even when he chooses to exercise his oversight through another bishop. Such an extension

should be seen as an expression of the collegiality of a House of Bishops which accepts both positions.

One may observe that what is missing here is a sense of stewardship, and a sense that the bishop is to be obeyed and followed because he is a faithful teacher and pastor who truly holds the faith once delivered to the saints. The faithful are not called to follow a bishop only because he fulfils the letter of canon law.

For there to be a truly open process of reception, testing, and discernment, diocesan bishops must be truly ready to accept the integrity of those who differ from them and in all charity make full provision for their pastoral needs. They need assistants to achieve this goal. It is easy to see why people begin to refer to the Provincial Episcopal Visitors [PEV], for example, as providing 'alternative oversight' rather than 'extended oversight'. In local reality, the PEV arrives as an alternative to the diocesan bishop because the parish does not wish to have the ministry of its ordinary, who ordains women.

It hardly needs to be stated here that this doctrine of the integrity of the bishop as ordinary will become exceedingly difficult to maintain if the Church of England moves forward to consecrate women as bishops. A female diocesan bishop would be forced to make tremendously difficult and painful decisions if she were to keep the process of reception moving in a free and open manner. It is probable that many would assume that the process is all but closed upon her arrival.

Working Party on Women in the Episcopate

At its July 2000 session the General Synod of the Church of England passed this resolution from Dr. Judith Rose, Archdeacon of Tonbridge:

That this Synod ask the House of Bishops to initiate further theological study on the episcopate, focussing on the issues that need to be addressed in preparation for a debate on women in the episcopate in the Church of England, and to make a progress report on this study to Synod in the next two years.

The House of Bishops established a working party, of which the chairman is the Bishop of Rochester, Michael Nazir-Ali. The Rochester Commission began work in April 2001 and made a progress report to the Synod in July 2002. Its planned work is in three stages: the theology of the episcopate, whether it is right to have women bishops, and the issue of communion in the event of women being consecrated as bishops. It is hardly possible, even in charity, to see the work of this group as a part of the open process of reception in the Church of England that provides aspects of testing and discernment for the Synod to consider. Rather, whatever the sincerity of its members and the value of papers emanating from its meetings, it appears to be a part of the undermining of the open process of reception, since it is actually discussing the proposal to minimise the testing of the reception of women's orders through the institution of the consecration of women bishops in the Church of England.

Therefore, it would appear either that the House of Bishops does not fully grasp the content of the process of reception, or that in grasping it, it does not intend strictly to conform to its demands and maintain the long and open process of testing and discernment according to the gospel that is the essence of Anglican receptionism, as defined by Anglicans for Anglicans.

Chapter Four:

Koinonia and the Anglican Family

A major argument of the Eames Reports (on maintaining communion in the Anglican family despite differences over women's ordination) and 1988 *The Virginia Report* (on the instruments of unity in the Anglican family of churches) is based upon the *koinonia* in God that is linked to *koinonia* in the church. As with the concept of reception, the concept of *koinonia,* as a dominant model for communion in God and between churches, has a background in ecumenical conversations, such as those between the Anglican Communion and others, including the Roman Catholic Church.

While these reports present practical advice and suggestions to the Anglican family, they also contain, as one would expect, certain theological presuppositions that serve as the basis for the advice. The most obvious and the most determinative of these theological principles is *koinonia,* a Greek word which in English Bibles is usually translated as 'communion' or 'fellowship'. This word occurs 13 times in the writings of the Apostle Paul (see e.g., 1 Cor 1:9; 2 Cor 13:13; Phil 1:5, etc.) and the related verb occurs 8 times. *Koinonia* also occurs in 1 John 1:3,6,7, and in Acts 2:42. For Paul, both the noun and verbal forms point to a new reality for sinful humans, and that reality is incorporation into the Lord Jesus Christ, into his death, resurrection, and glory, and thus into fellowship with him, and with the Father through him. It also includes incorporation into fellowship with all others who are united to Christ Jesus by the Holy Spirit in faith.

Still, *koinonia* is never used in the New Testament to indicate directly the internal life of the Triune God as a trinity of persons within the one Godhead. Neither is it used to describe the relationship of the eternal Father to the Lord Jesus Christ (the incarnate Son) or of the same incarnate Son to his Father. Further, it is not used for what theologians call the 'immanent Trinity' (God as he is unto, with, and towards himself in his own eternity, infinity, and glory) or for what is termed the 'economic Trinity' (God the Father as he is known by us in his self-revelation and in his relation to the world in creation and redemption through Jesus Christ and by the Holy Spirit). *Koinonia* is, however, used after the New Testament period by certain fathers of the church in relation to the Holy Trinity.

The Anglican Argument

Modern Anglican theologians, following hints in the tradition of the church and in the widespread ecumenical practice, use *koinonia* both for expressing the communion of the Father and the Lord Jesus Christ on earth, as well as the communion of the Father, the Son, and the Holy Spirit in the Holy Trinity—a unity in Trinity and a Trinity in unity. This usage is related to what is usually called a social doctrine of the Trinity, where the emphasis is upon community within God who is seen as a plurality in unity.

In these two reports, a major plea is made to maintain the unity and interdependence of the communion of churches on the basis of *koinonia* within 'the Triune God'. The argument asserts that as God is, so is the Anglican Communion as it mirrors him.

The basic thesis adopted in these Anglican reports, especially in *The Virginia Report* is that the *koinonia* (communion or fellowship) of the Anglican family of churches is grounded in the *koinonia* of the Holy Trinity, the triune God. This thesis may be summarised in the following way:

Communion (*koinonia*) exists eternally in the mutual relations of the Three Persons of the Holy Trinity, that is, between the Father and the Son, the Father and the Holy Spirit, the Son and the Holy Spirit. Autonomy is not an appropriate term to apply to any of three distinct Persons because there is a basic mutuality in and amongst the Three. There is a co-inherence of the three Persons in one another in the Holy Trinity, which makes any possibility of autonomy impossible. The Father is in the Son and the Son in the Father and the Holy Spirit in both. (Theologians have used the word *perichoresis* or *circuminsessio* (co-inherence) for this eternal mutuality and indwelling.)

The family of Anglican Churches participates by grace in the *koinonia* of the Holy Trinity so that there is actually a Communion of the Churches that is grounded in the Communion within the Holy Trinity. In the Communion of the Holy Trinity there is unity and diversity. In the Anglican Communion there is also unity and diversity—unity in baptismal faith and diversity in language, culture and doctrines.

Each Anglican province (or national church) is legally autonomous but like each Person of the Trinity, it is not to act in any way to deny the communion and the *perichoresis* in the diversity of Personhood within the single Godhead. Thus autonomy in the Anglican Family is always to be qualified by interdependency, especially in matters of major importance. Thus instruments of unity are extremely important in helping the communion of churches not only obey but also mirror God in his diverse plurality in unity.

Criticism of the Argument

1. The Anglican family of churches is only a small part of the one, holy, catholic and apostolic church. True *koinonia* belongs to the whole church of heaven and earth as a fellowship of members who are, as the body of Christ, united through the head, Christ Jesus, with the Father by the Holy Spirit. Therefore applying *koinonia* to any one part or jurisdiction of the divided church cannot be straightforward and must be problematic.

2. The *koinonia* that belongs to the Holy Trinity is not of the same essence (*ousia*, being or substance) as the *koinonia* that belongs to the body of Christ. The latter *koinonia* is not so much derived from the former but given freely, mercifully, and in a form appropriate to creatures.

3. The received doctrine or dogma of the Holy Trinity as created from scripture by the early church has two aspects or faces to it. As noted above, these are known as the 'immanent Trinity' (or God-as-he-is-unto-himself) and the 'economic Trinity' (or God-as-he-is-towards-us—in creation and salvation). Obviously, we know about the 'economic Trinity' from the revelation given to us of the Father and of the Son and of the Holy Spirit in the holy scriptures. What we know of the 'immanent Trinity' we know by deduction from what is revealed to us by God in grace as the 'economic Trinity.' However, to enter into this sphere of knowledge is to enter upon 'holy ground.' The New Testament describes the way in which the Father, through the Son and by the Holy Spirit, acts towards the world and us, and how we relate to the same Father through the Son and with the Holy Spirit. It says little as to the way that God is unto and with himself in the mystery of his Trinity and Unity. Here there is holy mystery, as we speak of that which is beyond our knowledge and

reason. We know little about the eternal and infinite *koinonia* of the Holy Trinity and we can say little of the co-inherence of the three persons. Yet we can stand back and adore the glory of the unity in Trinity and Trinity in unity.

4. What the Anglican argument from God's own unique *koinonia*, which we cannot truly know, to the special but limited *koinonia* of the Church seems to be doing is: (a) speaking with certainty about the 'immanent Trinity' (God-as-God-is-unto himself) as 'a unity in diversity' in a manner that is simplistic and tending to the secular, and, in so doing also confusing the 'immanent Trinity' with the 'economic Trinity' (God-as-he-is-towards us), and (b) basing the unity and diversity of the Anglican Communion (which is an empirical and changing reality) on this claimed (but faulty) knowledge of the Holy Trinity in his eternity and infinity. In so doing, it follows modern thinking which makes "diversity" a good thing and something that ought to be there in culture, society, education and government for its presence is necessary for the entity or society to be authentic and credible. However, properly speaking, diversity is truly a value-free term. It identifies a condition of unlikeness between or among things/people. It reports this difference as a fact and by itself indicates nothing of the goodness or badness of that fact. As a value-free term it is not appropriate to use of the Holy Trinity, for the Father, the Son and Holy Spirit, though different persons are also of the one and the same Being, substance or essence and so not, strictly speaking, diverse as such. As a modern secular term, it is also not appropriate to use it of the Holy Trinity because the difference between the eternal persons, a difference rooted in unity of Being, is greater than and like unto nothing which is celebrated as expressing diversity today.

5. The use of the blessed, holy and undivided Trinity of the Father, the Son and the Holy Spirit, as a model of unity in diversity to justify or to describe provinces, dioceses, or jurisdictions of the church is now common-place in Anglicanism. For example, in *Mission-Shaped Church*, a report to be received and debated at the February 2004 session of the Church of England's General Synod, diversity, like holiness and apostolicity, is presented as of the true nature of the church. In fact diversity is equated with 'catholicity' and, further, we are told that, "The Trinity provides the living example of unity in diversity", and "The diversity within unity of the one God provides a model for relationships between churches" (p.96). Here the holy of holies, the very essence of the Lord our God, appears to be invaded by secular thinking.

The Select Bibliography at the end of this booklet contains references for further reading on 'communion' within the church.

Comment

Alongside this official Anglican use, which in the Anglicanism of the global north is a relatively conservative use, there is a growing tendency to use the Trinity in more radical ways in, for example, ECUSA. It may be claimed that the Trinity is in vogue right now because progressive people have the idea that the Trinity amounts to a great mutuality of sharing, the sort that can be duplicated through people listening to each other and sharing their views and pain—and then doing the progressive thing anyway, in solemn piety!

In the Trinity, it appears, the Father, Son, and Holy Spirit exchange their truths with one another and experience a great harmony with one another. Their utopia can be our utopia if we only dialogue about it and feel it. It seems this Trinity has less and less to do with the God who is Lord. We need to get rid of all of that old God Almighty stuff and affirm that the whole cosmos is sharing and mutuality. God, it seems, has no law, no judgement—these are old and inadequate notions of God. We know now that he is pure relationship. Even identity is not all that important, because he can be a she or she can be a he and the Father can just as easily be a mother—anything goes. It seems clear that some progressives are going to do what they want to do under a thin 'Trinitarian' veneer. It is as if they can be orthodox and radically revisionist at the same time, and they see that as a bonus!

It may be stated that if the Archbishop of Canterbury's two Commissions (the Eames Commission and the Inter-Anglican Commission) had chosen a working model other than the Trinity with all its modern associations, then their work would have been very different indeed. Had they not worked from what may be termed a social doctrine of the Trinity (a concept widely used by theologians to criticise social and political structures they do not favour and to uphold the ones they do) but from, say, the model of order (*taxis*), and from the ordered hierarchy in the Trinity and the ordered complementarity of male and female, then they would have been open to the development not only of ordered but also hierarchical relations within the Church of God, with the bonus of *koinonia*. They also would have faced the question of the legitimacy of women's ordination and its reception very differently. Although order was a prominent theme in patristic and medieval times, as well as in the Reformation of the sixteenth century, it is hardly mentioned in these egalitarian days. A Trinity of mutuality of free persons is in vogue, where there are three autonomous persons in a voluntary relationship. This stands in great contrast to the profoundly complex unity of one substance, the *ousia*, shared by three co-inhering yet distinct persons.

However, we must deal with what the documents say, rather than what they could have said. We must say that the demands of genuine *koinonia* produced only by the Holy Spirit within the people of God are many and profound, and that they lay upon all members, from bishop to doorkeeper, the most serious responsibilities to live in love and peace with all fellow believers. *Koinonia*, in its Biblical presentation, does not depend upon being linked derivatively to a social doctrine of the Trinity and the concept of *koinonia* within the ineffable Holy Trinity. The teaching and exhortations of the books of the New Testament provide us with more than sufficient information and encouragement on how to live together in brotherly love, fellowship, and affection and why we must do so. Of course, this ethos will include the painful acts of discipline, rebuke, and exhortation. Yet whatever be the ecclesial situation and the controversies raging, the demands of *koinonia* and brotherly love never cease and are very clear to a common sense reader of the New Testament.

The need for such brotherly love, fellowship, and affection intensified during the summer of 2003 with the threats of schism and splits arising not only from the action of the General Convention of ECUSA in confirming an openly gay priest as the Bishop of New Hampshire, but also, in a lesser way, from evangelical intentions to introduce 'lay celebration' of the Holy Communion in the Diocese of Sydney.

In writing to the primates of the Anglican Communion on 23 July 2003, before the ECUSA decision, the Archbishop of Canterbury asked:

> But what does it mean to be a Communion [of Churches] rather than a federation? It means that provinces recognise each other as true

churches in Christ, so that the apostolic ministry of one local church can be exercised freely in another local church. It means that we have ways of being accountable to each other, so that decisions in any one local church are not taken without consultation and awareness of the consequences a decision may have for other churches. It means that we regard our unity as more than a matter of human agreement, more even that doctrinal uniformity; we see it as something rooted in the Word of God who is active both through our reading and hearing of Scripture and in our performance of the sacraments of Baptism and Confirmation.

On these criteria, the Anglican Communion is on the way to being a Communion, but still learning. Differences of belief about the ministry of women as priests and bishops have led us to a situation of impaired communion, in which the ministries of our provinces are not completely interchangeable. Our mutual accountability is still very undeveloped in regard to how we make decisions. What makes this a significant time in the Communion is that a number of the choices faced by provinces are choices that will clearly take us either nearer real communion or further from it.[1]

Dr. Williams ended by stating, "If we believe that our Anglican tradition has, by the grace of God, been given certain precious and life-giving elements for nourishing holy life and effective witness, we are bound by our duties and responsibilities as bishops to care for its survival and coherence." What binds the bishops surely also binds all of us, and what binds them is communion in truth and truth in communion.

---

[1] Full text available at http://www.cfdiocese.org/gencon/Rowan%207-23-03.htm (April 2004).

Chapter Five:

Observations and Suggestions

Let me begin by stating that I believe that the general guidelines for maintaining the highest level of communion during the time of testing and discernment for women's ordination are generally wise and should be followed by all, including the bishops, clergy, and people of the Church of England. This is true whether the guidelines are found in the original *Grindrod Report*, the reports of the Eames Commission and Eames Monitoring Group, or the Statements of the English House of Bishops (1993 and 2000). The guidelines should be followed despite what I think is an inappropriate use of the dogma of the blessed, holy, and undivided Trinity as the model for communion and fellowship.

However, since these guidelines and exhortations are set in the context of an open process of reception that is likely to be very long indeed (a fact often admitted in the literature of reception but rarely conceded in public speech), a question arises as to whether there is the stamina to be patient not for months, but for years, perhaps decades, especially amongst those who favour the ordination of women. Certainly unless bishops—in particular those who ordain women—firmly take the initiative to inform their flocks that the process is long and ongoing, then there is great danger of continued attempts to bring the process to a hasty conclusion. People in the local parish must understand that the process of discernment requires mutual understanding, respect, and charity. The desire for and the organisation of the Working Party on Women in the Episcopate has been seen in this light by some. There would not be any need for this working party had there been a vital, practical commitment to the received concept of reception in its modern Anglican form, rather than mere lip service paid to it.

In fact, bringing what should be a long and open process to a hasty conclusion has already officially taken place in ECUSA, where in 2000 the General Convention made acceptance of women's ordination mandatory for office holders, lay and clerical. Then the Convention sent out official visiting parties to certain dioceses to examine their commitment to this process and to seek to bring them into line if their progress was less than satisfactory. It is also happening unofficially in several places in Canada, Great Britain, and Australia, where opponents of women's ordination believe that they are not being treated as full members of a diocese or province.

Let us be honest. Too often in the northern provinces of the Anglican Communion the concept of reception is used by those who favour the ordination of women solely as a means of gaining space, respect, honour, and preferment for ordained women in the churches. In other words, the primary value of the concept for them, so it would appear, is its emphasis on maintaining good relations during the period of reception and discernment, not so that the cause of women's ordained ministry may be truly tested or its nature rightly discerned, but that it should prosper. They are motivated by sincere beliefs that the right of women to exercise ordained ministry is so compelling that they are ready to push it in all possible ways.

In contrast, those who oppose the innovation of women presbyters and bishops in the global north usually end up pleading for toleration, for respect, for their candidates for holy orders to be taken seriously, and for the elevation of some of their numbers to senior positions such as bishops, diocesan and suffragan. They are often found as a minority calling for human rights! Such a situation is not one where the open process of reception in ongoing *koinonia* is being exercised in the Holy Spirit for the sake of the honour of Jesus Christ our Lord.

One worrying aspect of the current use of the concept of reception, especially in ECUSA, is its transfer from the realm of women's ordination (for which it was designed by the *Grindrod Report*) to the blessing of same-sex partnerships and the ordination of active homosexuals. Since these innovations now have synodical approval from ECUSA's General Convention and are in place and are developing, some Episcopalians are claiming that these ecclesiastical acts are an inevitable part of the process of reception, even though at this stage there appears to be world-wide condemnation of them.

The Church of England and Reception

Let us now turn our attention specifically to the Church of England and to the work of the Rochester Commission on Women in the Episcopate, a commission that is ongoing as this essay is being written and published.

It would seem that little serious thought is given anywhere in the Church of England to answering this question: *on what reasonable grounds is it possible to think of moving ahead to the consecration of women when the very fact of the ordination of women as presbyters and their deployment in parishes is still a matter of an open process of reception for testing and discernment in the Church of England?* It is important to recall that when the Church of England and the British Parliament approved the ordaining of women, it was actually the ordaining of them as deacons and presbyters (priests), not as bishops. In fact, the ordination and consecration of women as bishops was specifically excluded from the canonical legislation and parliamentary approval. This is why, ten years later and with ten years of reception activity completed, there is a working party, chaired by the Bishop of Rochester, looking into its possibility.

This is not the appropriate place to rehearse the arguments from scripture, tradition, and reason against the innovation of ordaining women as priests and bishops, for these have been made elsewhere in books, articles, and essays, in presentations to the working party, and with clarity and brevity by the Ecclesiastical Committee of Parliament in its Report on the 1993 Priests (Ordination of Women) Measure. It is, however, the place to state and to argue that on the basis of the process of reception, the Church of England, and its bishops in particular, ought not to proceed in the direction of enlarging the innovation of ordaining women. I use the verbal form 'ought' because I see it as a moral obligation.

The fact of the matter is that their own commitment to the process of reception as expounded so eloquently in the Manchester Statements of 1993 truly precludes the moving to the consecration of women as bishops in the near future. In truth, it prevents moving forward for a long time, until the testing and discernment are completed. Even then, as they have conceded in writing, the result at the end of the open process may be a judgement that the experiment has been partially or even wholly misguided.

If we are to be precise, the House of Bishops committed itself to the process of reception with regard only to the placing of women in the first two orders of the threefold ministry. It never stated clearly and unambiguously (or even vaguely) that the process of reception really applied to the reception of all three orders, but that in the case of the Church of England it was only being temporarily applied to the first two orders. All of its teaching in its various reports and statements from 1992 to 1994, and then again in 2000, concerned the process of reception with regard to women as presbyters, and as presbyters only. Further, the Canon Law of the Church of England specifically prohibits a woman being consecrated to the office of bishop (see Canon C2).

Now it is true that in other provinces (in New Zealand and North America) women have been consecrated as bishops; however, because of provincial autonomy, and especially the unique autonomy of established Church of England, what has happened in other provinces carries no authority whatsoever in the Church of England. The House of Bishops is currently committed to testing the innovation and experiment of ordaining women to the first two orders, and to these alone. For the House to add women in the third order to this complex state of affairs of testing and discernment would be, I believe, to act dishonestly, hastily, and prematurely, and to contradict its own clear words. I believe that what I state remains true even if the Rochester Commission reports that the theological arguments in favour of elevating women to the episcopate are compelling (that is, compelling as they are seen at this point of time in the life of the church and the situation in western culture where the dignity of women is emphasised). A commitment to reception has been made and it must, on moral and theological grounds, be adhered to and allowed to be an open process.

The argument against this strong position can be, and will be, stated in various ways. One way would be to argue that the concept of reception as expounded in the Eames Commission and earlier by *The Grindrod Report* had specific reference to women in the episcopate. Thus, the full context of novel Anglican exposition of reception was already set before the

House of Bishops and the General Synod adopted this concept for their own pastoral and political purposes. Even though the leadership of the Church of England did not refer to women as bishops (for obvious reasons) in their documents and legislation during 1992 and 1993, the fact that some bishops were women was the remote context. (It is worth recalling that in the 1988 *Second Report of the House of Bishops on the Ordination of Women to the Priesthood*, the bishops discussed women bishops and were against the idea.) So, ten years later in a different climate, that remote context can be recalled and made the primary context, and therefore the innovation of women bishops can be added to the other two orders wherein women have been admitted, and the process of testing and discernment can begin in full swing and the real thing, the threefold ministry of women, can be the subject of reception in the church.

In response, I state that the Church of England began its own form of testing and discernment ten years ago, and that this ongoing process should not be interrupted by what would be a very major change in the life of the national church. There are now in place the structures and the guidelines, not to mention the experience, for allowing the process of reception to proceed in a reasonable, convivial, and mature way, and thus for true discernment and testing to take place. Whatever would be the individual holiness and charm of a woman bishop, her presence as a female bishop would seriously disturb the present fragile means of maintaining a basic level of communion, respect, and integrity, and would make extremely difficult the continuation of the open process of reception. The calls for a Third Province would intensify, and the Church of England would probably enter into a legalised form of internal schism.

If the Church of England wants to gather information about how women bishops are received and how their ministry is tested, there are the 'experiments' in North America and New Zealand to monitor, even though in these cases the provinces in question (and thus the contexts of ministry) are not national, established churches as is the Church of England. While there remains a vocal, well-informed, and theologically literate minority (evangelicals, anglo-catholics and others) who oppose the ordination of women to the presbyterate and episcopate either on biblical, theological, or ecumenical principles, it cannot be said that the process of reception is complete. In fact, it must be admitted that it is still ongoing, and so testing and discernment must surely continue. Further, this is also the case in the vast majority of the 38 provinces of the Anglican Communion, and understanding the process of reception in the right way involves taking into account what is happening in the whole Anglican communion.

Therefore, rather than pressing for the consecration of women as bishops, the House of Bishops and the General Synod ought to be making clear to all the proper context of fellowship and mutuality within which people of different opinions can live together in reasonable harmony as they patiently engage in testing and discernment of this innovation. In other words, the House of Bishops should recall its own teaching of 1993 and of 2000 in published documents and seek to lead the church to accept it and follow it. It should remind its flocks of the fact that 'the process of reception in the Church can be difficult and time-consuming; there is no pre-determined result.'

To conclude this section, some words from *The Virginia Report*, received and adopted by the Lambeth Conference of 1998, are appropriate:

Anglicans hold that the universal Church will not ultimately fail. Through the leading of the Holy Spirit, truth is gradually discerned. However, the discernment of truth is never an uncomplicated and straightforward matter. There are always setbacks along the way.

Within the Anglican Communion matters which touch the communion of all the churches need to be discerned and tested within the life of the interdependence of the Provinces, through the meeting of bishops in the Lambeth Conference and through the consultative process of the Anglican Consultative Council and the Primates' Meeting. Beyond that lies the process of open reception within the life of the local churches. The maintenance of communion both within and between churches, in the process of testing the truth of a decision needs great sensitivity, and adequate space needs to be found for clearly expressed dissent in testing and refining truth. In the process of discernment and reception relationships need to be maintained, for only in fellowship is there an opportunity for correcting one-sidedness or ignorance. Though some of the means by which communion is expressed may be strained, the need for courtesy, tolerance, mutual respect, prayer for one another and a continuing desire to know and be with one another, remain binding upon us as Christians. (p.41)

In the process of open reception, I would add, the Church of England is not yet ready for the introduction of female bishops, even if it is desired by the majority. There is still a long way to go on the difficult road of testing and discernment of open reception.

A further consideration

The doctrinal foundation of the Church of England is based upon the sacred canon of holy scriptures. The Church of England's faith is set forth in the Catholic creeds and in its historic formularies—the Articles of Religion, the Book of Common Prayer, and the Ordering of Bishops, Priests and Deacons (the Ordinal). Thus, if we want to know the doctrine of the Church of England concerning the ordained ministry we go to the scriptures and to the Ordinal.

The formularies are written in that form of language that is usually called 'traditional language' but which I prefer to call 'the English language of prayer' (see Toon and Tarsitano, *Neither Archaic nor Obsolete*). One of the features of this language is that man often means 'man and woman' and 'he' often means 'male or female.' Thus it has been often noticed that within the style and logic of the language of *The Book of Common Prayer*, the service for the Ordaining of Priests can actually be used of women without any violation of that language, and this is so even though only men were envisaged as candidates for this office in 1549, 1552, 1559, 1604, and 1662, when the Prayer Book was published and the Ordinal printed with it. In fact, in the Canons of the Church of England, we read: "In the forms of service contained in the Book of Common Prayer or in the Ordinal words importing the masculine gender in relation to the priesthood shall be construed as including the feminine, except where the context otherwise requires" (Canon C4B, No. 2).

The same, however, cannot be said of the service 'The Form of Ordaining or Consecrating of an Archbishop or Bishop'. Here the style of the language is such that it can only mean that it is a man who is a candidate for consecration. For example, the bishop-elect is presented to the Archbishop with these words: 'Most reverend Father in God, we present unto you this godly and well-learned man to be ordained and consecrated Bishop.' Here the Archbishop, as a member of the House of Lords, is addressed in the appropriate way as 'you' rather than 'thee' (cf. 'your grace' and 'your majesty') and the candidate is called 'this godly and well-learned man,' not 'person.' Further, in the Litany is placed this suffrage: 'That it may please thee [God] to bless this our Brother elected, and to send thy grace upon him...' Here the natural meaning is that a man is being prayed for. What this use of language means is that the content of the service for the consecrating of a bishop would have to be modified in order to make this official formulary allow the consecrating of a woman priest as a bishop. Unlike the service for ordaining priests, this service does not by a reasonable interpretation of its use of nouns and male pronouns allow the consecration of a woman.

Thus to move forward and to consecrate a woman presbyter as a woman bishop requires the Church of England to change one of its formularies. In this context, it is worth recalling that the ECUSA 1979 Prayer Book (which is still ECUSA's official formulary) contains a revised Ordinal which uses 'he/she' and thus can be used, as it was clearly intended, both for the ordination of women as priests and the consecration of women as bishops. However, the introduction of this revised Prayer Book meant ECUSA setting aside and rejecting the historic formularies. I hope that the Church of England seeks neither to change the formulary nor to pretend that the formulary does not teach what it does teach.

In Conclusion

The Anglican Communion of churches historically arose from the Church of England. The Church of England thus has the privilege and duty to set an example to the other 37 provinces on maintaining common life in holiness and in truth. If it truly has accepted the process of reception and takes seriously what its bishops have declared concerning this process, then it must lead the way first in showing the necessary restraint in not moving forward with women's consecration, and second by exercising the magnanimous charity of true *koinonia* and fellowship to all its members. It must not behave as if the Anglican family is merely a federation of churches, with each one glorying in its autonomy and seeking communion with others only for secondary reasons.

Let the Church of England practice what it has preached and lead the way in discovering and exhibiting the possibilities of the full meaning of the concept of reception. No other province of the Anglican family has used so fully the concept in its public documents when introducing the ordination of women as has the Church of England, and so no other province has the unique opportunity to demonstrate in practise and in the expositions of its teachers and theologians what testing and discernment are all about!

SELECT BIBLIOGRAPHY

Reports and Documents

A Second Report, The House of Bishops GS 829 (London: Church House Publishing, 1988).

Being in Communion, GS Misc 418 (London: Church House Publishing, 1993).

Bonds of Peace, GS 1074 (London: Church House Publishing, 1993).

Episcopal Ministry Act of Synod: Report of a Working Party of the House of Bishops, GS Misc 1395 (London: Church House Publishing, 2000).

Manchester Statement (Statement by the House of Bishops following its meeting in Manchester, January 1993: reproduced in the 203rd Report of the Houses of Parliament Ecclesiastical Committee on the Church of England, Priests (Ordination of Women) Measure 1993, No. 2, pp.21-23).

Mission-Shaped Church: Church Planting and Fresh Expressions of Church in a Changing Context, GS 1523 (London: Church House Publishing, 2004).

Report on Mission and Ministry, The Lambeth Conference 1988 (London: Church House Publishing, 1988).

The Book of Common Prayer, 'The Form and Manner of Making Ordaining and Consecrating of Bishops, Priests and Deacons According to the Order of the Church of England', 1662.

The Eames Commission: The Official Reports. The Archbishop of Canterbury's Commission on Communion and Women in the Episcopate (Toronto: Anglican Book Centre, 1994).

The Gift of Authority: Authority in the Church III, Anglican - Roman Catholic International Commission (ARCIC) (London: Catholic Truth Society, 1999).

The Ordination of Women to the Priesthood: A Report by the House of Bishops, GS 764 (London: Church House Publishing, 1987).

The Truth Shall Make You Free: The Lambeth Conference: Reports, Resolutions and Pastoral Letters from the Bishops (London: Church House Publishing, 1988).

The Virginia Report: The Report of the Inter-Anglican Theological and Doctrinal Commission (Harrisburg, PA: Morehouse, 1999).

Together in Mission and Ministry: The Porvoo Common Statement with Essays on Church and Ministry in Northern Europe (London: Church House Publishing, 1993).

Women and the Episcopate: The Grindrod Report (London: Anglican Consultative Council, 1988).

Women in the Anglican Episcopate: Theology Guidelines and Practice. The Eames Commission and the Monitoring Group Reports (Toronto: Anglican Book Centre, 1988).

Working Party on Women in the Episcopate: A Progress Report (London: Church House Publishing, 2002).

Other Publications

Avis, P. (2003) (ed.) <u>Seeking the Truth of Change in the Church: Reception, Communion and the Ordination of Women</u> London: T&T Clark.

Best, T.F. & Gassman, G. (1994) (eds) <u>On the Way to Fuller Communion</u> Geneva: World Council of Churches.

Chadwick, H. (1997) <u>Reception</u> in Sugden, C. & Samuel, V. (eds) *Anglican Life and Witness: A Reader for the Lambeth Conference of Anglican Bishops 1998* London: SPCK (pp.200ff).

Coleman, R. (1992) (ed.) <u>Resolutions of the Twelve Lambeth Conferences 1867-1988</u> Toronto: Anglican Book Centre.

Congar, Y. (1972) <u>Reception as an Ecclesiological Reality</u> in Albergio, G. & Weiler, A. (eds) *Election and Consensus in the Church* New York: Herder & Herder.

Doyle, D.M. (2000) <u>Communion Ecclesiology: Vision and Versions</u> Maryknoll, NY: Orbis Books.

Evans, G.R. (1990) <u>Authority in the Church: a Challenge for Anglicans</u> Norwich: Canterbury Press.

Gomez, D.W. & Sinclair, M.W. (2001) (eds) <u>To Mend the Net: Anglican Faith and Order for Renewed Mission</u> Carrolton, TX: Ekklesia Society.

Healey, N.M. (2000) <u>Church, World and the Christian Life: Practical-Prophetic Ecclesiology</u> Cambridge: Cambridge University Press.

Rusch, W.B. (1988) <u>Reception: An Ecumenical Opportunity</u> Philadelphia: Fortress Press.

Tanner, M. (1990) <u>Reception and Provisionality among Anglicans</u> *Mid-Stream* 29 (pp.51ff.).

Tillard, J.M.R. (1992) <u>Church of Churches: The Ecclesiology of Communion</u> Collegeville, MN: Liturgical Press.

Tillard, J.M.R. (1992) Reception—Communion *One in Christ* 28 (pp.307ff.).

Toon, P. & Tarsitano, L.R. (2003) Neither Archaic Nor Obsolete: The Language of Common Prayer and Public Worship Denton, Norfolk: Edgeways Books.

Toon, P. (1979) The Development of Doctrine in the Church Grand Rapids, MI: Eerdmans.

Toon, P. (2003) Common Worship Considered: A Liturgical Journey Examined Denton, Norfolk: Edgeways Books.

Volf, M. (1998) After our Likeness: The Church as the Image of the Trinity Grand Rapids, MI: Eerdmans.

Zizioulas, J. (1985) The Theological Problem of Reception *One in Christ* 21 (pp.190ff.).